A Phoenix & Her Ashes

CƷ℞

A Phoenix
& Her Ashes

Sarkis Kavaris

DEDICATION

For my grandmothers, Dawn and Rose, for their enduring spirit and courage; without whose love, wisdom, and guidance, this book would likely never have been written.

And for all the grace I've discovered within my own life, in all its forms presented to me. And for all the times I have recognized it as such–I am eternally grateful.

TABLE OF CONTENTS

Preface

I hope this book find you, and finds you well.
The following collection of poetry and prose
aims to weave a tapestry of meaning, gleaned
from everyday experiences. It is at its core, an
honest and vulnerable attempt to try and find the
extraordinary in the seemingly ordinary; to make
sense of elements that seem, on the surface, to
be devoid of reason, while trying to discover
inspiration as much and as often as permissible.
It is an honest, unapologetic exploration into the
themes of love, pain, forgiveness, and growth
bestowed upon us by the healing balms of grace.

It is my hope that this book inspires you in some
small way, as it has for me. Thank you for your
time, because really, that is the greatest gift you
can offer to any writer—your precious time.

Best Wishes Always,
Sarkis

ON LOVE & LOVING

fleeting memories

If all we are, is
but a series of fleeting memories,
an array of moments
fluttering past one another
in an endless sea of happenstance,
like vivid pulsations of light
propelling themselves through the cosmos,
then maybe the phrase
"I love you"
really means:

this moment within me
         embraces
                  this moment within you.

souls

Because one soul meets another
long before any words are uttered,
any prayers wished upon,
or any frequencies exchanged.

Before thought becomes action,
mind evolves into consciousness,
breath into air–
they first meet one another
in the infinite spaces
in between.

Souls do have mates,
after all.

the answer

The answer is always
undeniably,
indisputably,
unequivocally…
love.

***

Sometimes, we tend to overanalyze a given
situation.

It's important to remember that even though the
questions may appear to be complex, the answer
rarely is.

the ultimate task

The ultimate task
& ultimate lesson,
is to unlearn all of the fear
we have learned and to accept
love as the final and only answer
to all of the questions
we may have ever asked
in this lifetime
and the next.

a grandmother's dream

And it's finally clear to me now,
after all these years,
that during all those dark, harrowed nights
when I couldn't dream (for myself),
you dreamt for me.

And that really made all the difference…

***

For my late grandmother.

Because I often find myself reminiscing
about the love she expressed to me.
And as I've lived,
I've recognized that same love
in all things good and beautiful
in this world.

Not a day goes by when I don't remember your
kind and generous spirit, the way you radiated
love in all that you said and did, the grace that
permeated through you and into others' lives. I
often recall the laughter we shared, my young
hopes that I would confide in you. You nurtured
those hopes, as if they were your own.

I simply did not know it at the time, but during all those dark nights when I was too scared to dream, you were dreaming for me all along. Thank you, Nene.

love is eternal

There are moments in life
when the world needs to hear your voice.
        It just does.

So don't be afraid.
Much like how a flower needs its sustenance
of sunlight, water and soil,
the universe beckons to hear your voice.

And in those moments,
the universe listens to you:
for you to make that difference it so needs.
The stars align to create a channel
for your message to travel,
        to the depths of the ether.

The land settles in peace as you speak.
And the goodness that spreads
permeates into all the beings
that inhabit the earth–
plants, trees, humans, animals.

They are forever affected
by your word, by your touch, by your actions.
Life will endure,
but it may only prosper if you contribute
to it's goodness.

Love is eternal.

goodness, wherever

Spread love
and goodness,
wherever you may go,
& wherever life finds you.

***

I learned from a very young age, that we all
possess a certain amount of goodness, inside.
And it's in learning how to spread that goodness
found within each one of us, that we feel deeply
alive.

Perhaps it's in knowing that it is possible for us
to influence another being in a positive way, no
matter how small; it is this possibility that
matters to us, that means something to us.

May we all learn what it truly means to give
parts of ourselves away to another, with no hope
of getting them back, so that he or she too can
pay it forward. And onwards, like tiny ripples in
a vast ocean, the trend may continue. It is
through such seemingly small, arbitrary actions
that the world may change for the better.

utopia

Of all the utopias that may exist,
among all the variances
and differing permutations of lives to be lived
and breaths to be taken,
I've fallen in love with the one
in which you and I
bless each other's insecurities to death
until they are vanished forever.

And we are left as what we've always been,
love being aware of itself in another.

love comes back around

The journey is all about love–
the love you've given away
        &
the love you've received.
They are both one in the same.

***

Love comes back around…always. All the love
you've ever given away, in time, will journey its
way back to you. That's just how the universe
works. Like energy, love cannot be created or
destroyed. In this manner, the love that existed
from generations past still lives on within us and
through us.

bricks & souls

True love
doesn't meet you
at your best.

It finds you
at your worst,
holds you patiently by the hand,
and builds you up:

brick by brick,
soul to soul.

believe in love

I want to believe
in the light of the world
or nothing at all,

believe in love
or nothing at all–

because without love,
life is meaningless;
and without meaning,
life is loveless.

the grace within you

Grace is a peculiar thing.
You only realize it exists
in the stillness;
it rises up

quietly,
out of nowhere,
unassuming and ever present.

It makes its way inside you,
and builds a home within your bones;
your soul, a fortress.
You finally feel you belong.

Heaven isn't only a place,
an endpoint,
an afterthought.
It also resides within you.
And grace is your companion
in reaching to discover it.

I was looking for my way back home, when I
finally realized: I was already home, all along.

synergy

The greatest forms of relationship
are those characterized by synergy–
when the union of two people
creates an entity
or energy
greater than the sum of its parts.

These are the relationships
that move mountains
and appease storms,

that change the meaning
of things long-forgotten,
misunderstood,
forged in stone.

That create life anew.

it was love, all along

And all along,
love was all
you were ever made of:
pure,
unconditional,
all-encompassing
love.

two into one

Because everything you've ever experienced,
you've really lived through twice:
once with your head
and once with your heart.

And if you're in true alignment,
they both become one.

the reflections of wonder

I have always been
forever in awe,
at the world within
and without.

Like a mirror,
an infinite reflection,
the light within our souls
greets the light of the universe.
We share the same light,
and the same soul.
We both are one.

The language of eternity
needs no formal introduction.
We are well-versed in it,
in the words of wonder.

st. valentine

Radiate love
to such a degree
& in such a way,
that even St. Valentine
would be proud.

love myself

But most of all
you've taught me to love myself.
Just as you have loved me.

I'm slowly discovering who I am,
entering into locked rooms
to which you've already found the key.
It's like you knew me,
before I even knew myself.

the wrinkles of soulmates

One morning, I took a stroll to a nearby park. As I walked along the cobblestone pathway carved through the patches of wilderness, I witnessed an elderly couple–most likely well into their 80's–sitting hand-in-hand on a nearby bench. The scene itself was one easily gleaned from a romantic movie.

The gentleman was making his Mrs., laugh. It was the kind of laughter that was soft and barely audible from where I was standing. He was telling her stories, without even glimpsing at her reactions.

He had memorized them all. He didn't need to look.

And so he continued animating these tales to life, until suddenly he stopped. He then ran his index and middle fingers gently across her forehead, and pressed it neatly between her wrinkles. Each crevice in her flesh engulfed the warm embrace of his fingertips, if only for a moment. And I realized, at that moment, that he wasn't just feeling her wrinkles…but also his own. For the very same wrinkles adorning her forehead, her cheek, her jaw, they also were present on his.

He wanted to feel how long they had been together. How far they had traveled, together. He wanted to visit each trial and tribulation they had faced over the years, and how they had fallen together–only to rise again, together.

And as his fingers continued to press gently, he knew she was the one: she had always been. For only when your wrinkles align to match those of another, do you know you have found your true soulmate.

particles of love

I am millions of particles
in vibrational synchrony,
quivering in a dream-like trance,
in a 3-dimensional paradigm
disguised as me and my meaning (heretofore).
And all of them
are radiating
the colors of love.

centuries of lovers

Lovers don't meet by chance,
but by design.
They rarely cross paths by accident.
Their meeting was always destined to occur;
and their paths were etched
centuries ago in the stars.

alchemy

There are special people in your life
that are able to change the meaning of certain
memories you've held onto for years,

meanings of things you thought
would never change.

They are able to take the negative associations
you've built around an experience,
a place, an idea,
hold them gently within their hands,
allow their light
to heal and transform and mold
them into something new.

In this way, they are able
to turn back the years, and change
ugliness into beauty,
darkness into light,
shame into pride.

Don't ever let go of these special people.

for nene 1.0

There are some people in this world who are born with something special. A little something extra.

From a very young age, they are blessed with a peculiar sense of self. Of who they are and how it is they wish to live their lives.

These are the sorts of people for whom books are written, and stories passed down from generation to generation.

In time they become legends. Heroes, even.

Beautiful embodiments of love.

These people inhabit this world, but really operate as if they are living in another; they behave differently. They live their ideals in the 'here and now,' because they know that these are the important principles to live by, to live for–principles like: loving and forgiving others, being kind to all beings who are breathing and are possessing of life.

These individuals realize from a very young age that what truly matters is the difference you have made in the life of another. That everything else is miniscule in comparison, because you can't take any of it, any of it, with you.

This is the kind of person my grandmother was. You see, during her entire lifetime, she was residing on earth, but was living as if she was already in Heaven.

She was born into her own Heaven.

But only she knew this. We didn't. Until now.

It is the ultimate riddle she left us with. How can someone be so kind and nurturing to everyone here on earth? But that's just it; she never really was on earth. She was in Heaven all along.

Welcome home, Nene.

like wildfire

The soul,
the soul will always remain intact.
The soul is love,
and love, like wildfire
is indestructible.

our love story

If ours was a love story,
it would end
the same way it began:
amid smiles and laughter,
the warm embrace of twilight
incandescing its shadows upon us,
paying homage to our past,
our souls intertwined for eternity
as we walk each other home.

ashes onto ashes

The warmth,
softly seducing the cold, crisp night.
Gentle fingers
rubbing on flesh;

the palms of our hands,
damp and dripping
mixing with the oceans,
rivers streaming through our lifelines.

A dizzy dance.
Internal combustion,
pressure cooker, steam and sound,
the fury. The light swallows the darkness.
Silence.
Silence is born.

A phoenix and new beginnings.

ON PAIN & SORROW

railroads

She had a habit
of taking photos at railroad stations.
They just felt like home.

Maybe because
she never had one to call her own,
or perhaps because she hated commitment
or the idea of it.

She feared it.
And don't we all just hate
what we fear the most?

She longed to be able to disappear
at a moment's notice.
Just to leave it all behind,
for once.
Not to run away,
but just to leave
the life she knew behind,
and to start fresh,
in a place

without any railroads...

memories of goodbye

The saddest part of goodbye
isn't the 'leaving-behind,'
but rather
it's the replacement of memories.
Like the contents in a jar,
you can only store so much.

So as you move forward in life
and create new memories,
the old ones you've held onto so dearly
& protected from the decays of daylight,
are displaced
& forgotten.

Like a lost language
or a mummified artifact.

And what was once so familiar and inviting,
all of a sudden becomes foreign,
even alienating.

That's what hurts the most,
because here's the thing:

*I don't want to forget you,
not just yet...*

we fall to rise

We fall
not simply to rise up,
but because there was something
down there
we were meant to find.

*And we are only able to rise
when we find it.*

May we all find the grace we need,
precisely when we need it the most.

the questions

Sometimes,
you don't get all the answers;
you're left with the questions.

Because sometimes,
just sometimes,

the questions themselves
are far more important.

the flames of destiny

These challenges you're going through,
they are meant to help you grow;
to mature into the person
you were meant to be.

How else will you learn to withstand
the tortuous grips of a hurricane,
when you cannot even bear
the most gentle of caresses
from an ocean breeze?

How else will you learn to stand
tall and proud
in mind, body, and soul
amidst the roaring
of life's unforgiving rapids,
whilst you wilt and break
with every rub and nudge
from a trickle of water?

To withstand the flame,
you must be engulfed by the flame,
become the flame,
and rise from within the flame.

pieces

Once apart, rarely
do the pieces fit
back together
the way they
once did--

and maybe they were never meant to
in the first place.

borne to burn

Because some stars
just burn too damn bright.
Their incandescence
belongs to a world not of our own.
They are borne to burn,
simply to return
to the place from which
they originated.
And our loss
becomes heaven's gain.
Our darkness,
heaven's light.

And one thing is for certain:
Heaven became so much richer,
for it gained an angel.

finding happiness

"And after all of this,
will I ever find happiness
once again?"

She replied,
"happiness is waiting for you.
It's always been waiting for you;
but here's the thing–
you've got it all wrong."

"You don't find happiness,
it finds you. It always finds you."

the flourishes of fear

In order to flourish,
you need to go and visit
the places within you
that you fear the most,
and make them a home.

911

He explained to us how, in the middle of the night, he felt a sharp pain jolting across his forearm, cutting like a serrated knife through the tendons in his arm, all the way to his elbow.

They rushed him to the ER. It was a blood clot.

Had he waited any longer, the clot could have traveled to his brain or his lungs. The former is a stroke; the latter, a pulmonary embolism. Both of which are fatal.

And as he stood there before us, my mind kept drifting back to the pain he felt, and how the pain was his cue to call for help. It had basically saved his life, for it triggered the 911 call.

The pain had served a purpose in his life.

***

And then I thought about the emotional pain we all endure as human beings: all the flavors of death and loss–loss of self and loss of friends.

And I thought to myself, can this pain also serve a purpose? Can we find meaning in the struggle?

When our hearts begin to palpate and ache, is it a sign or a call for something we should do, an action we should take? Or a lesson we should learn?

Perhaps we are being taught something.

Pain has a way of teaching you at a faster rate than most other things in life. It can be your best teacher, if you let it. But only if you move through the pain. And the only way to move through it is just that–through it.

You need to sit with it.

Be present in its presence.

Be mindful of what it is that hurts.

And why it hurts the way it does?

Make the pain your friend.

Have a picnic date with it. And don't forget to bring the milk and cookies.

Let it be your teacher, and you the student.

There is much it can teach you, but only if you are ready to listen, and ready to receive its blessings.

from chaos, beauty

And the irony is this:
in order to grow,
you need to be willing to break.

Out of the chaos,
the ashes will achieve
a sort of synchrony,
and true beauty will emerge.

problem-solving 101

I know it sounds weird, and I know it may sound counterintuitive, but at a particular point, you cannot solve certain problems by focusing directly upon them any longer. No amount of brainstorming, strategizing, problem-solving, or analyzing will change anything, let alone the nature of the problem.

The solution to some problems lies in simply taking a break from them, and thinking about them. A 'mini-vacation' of sorts. They are solved literally by focusing on other things, by investing your energy into the people, places, events, and passions that light the fire within you, and the vastness of your imagination without you.

And somehow, gradually over time, you miraculously find the answers to these problems without even knowing that you've been working upon them all along. They just come to you; they appear before you as a kind of pleasant surprise, out of the blue. You may wonder, in the moment, how in the world this happened, but really it was your doing all along.

This entire time, you've just been living your way into the answers, without even knowing it.

You just needed time and space. That's all it takes sometimes: time and space.

Sometimes, the energy you invest in certain parts of your life, comes back to you in the form of answers you've been seeking to problems in other parts of your life. It's a funny thing how that works.

Like I said, it's counterintuitive, really.

the things they can't take away

The things
they cannot change,
the parts within you
they cannot take away,
are the very things
you need to nurture.

These are the things that stay
and make you who you are.
In time, they become the elements in your life,
that create meaning out of suffering,
love out of darkness.

gifts from darkness

Some gifts,
you need the darkness
to help you find.

They reside
and are blessed
in the dissonance,
where no light may reach,
where fear roams free,
among the flurries of fury,

waiting to be discovered.

***

The answer to your prayers,
that gift seemingly brought to you
out of the darkness,
was inside you all along.
You just needed the darkness
in order to help you find it.

deserve

Always remember.
You deserve all of the things
you were ever denied,
long before you were ever denied them.

Don't you ever forget that.

pomegranate free flows

Tell me–
when a pomegranate falls
from the branches of its embryonic home
from where it belongs
endures the free fall ricochet through the skies
and catapults itself into the dense soil below,
does she feel any pain?

Does she feel any hurt?
Does she question her existence?
Does she blame life for her journey?
If so, what would she say?
How would she respond?

The journey is all about love:
love you've received
and love you've given away
Because even in the most unlikely of places,
the most dire of circumstances,
love finds a way.

In terror camps and fields of genocide,
love finds a way.

In the incessant suffering of the minds' eye,
love finds a way.

In those heartbreakers of sorrow and defeat,
love finds a way.

In losses unimaginable and irreversible,
love finds a way.

In the killings and torture of the innocent,
love finds a way.

In the terrors of murder
and unspeakable violence,
love finds a way.

In the hunger of children
walking naked in the desert,
love finds a way.

In the bullets and cold daggers
that pierce the warm flesh
and ooze out whatever is inside,
love finds a way.

In the evil that attempts
to break and obliterate the spirit,
love finds a way.

In moments of doubt and uncertainty,
love finds a way.

In the seemingly-glaring absence
of the holy ghost,
love finds a way.

The journey is all about love:

love you've given away
and love you've received.

The pomegranate knows this;
she does not question it.

She knows that
the healing is in the fall.
Her healing lies in the fall.
She does not blame the fall,
because she knows
the healing is in the fall.

The pomegranate
does not question her journey
because she knows that the fall
is part of the journey–
her journey into love.
It's part of it all.
There is a purpose to the free flow,
to the mystery,
to love.

There is always a purpose to love.

eyes of gratitude

The real beauty
in facing certain challenges in your life
are the people that come to your aid
to help and support you.

They are the people
who possess a strong love for you,
who will not let you fall,
who remind you of your worth
when you have long-forgotten,
who rise to the occasion,
time and again
and help you through
tumultuous times.

These are your angels,
sent to guide you
through this charade
we call life;
and you can really only be
full of gratitude and love
for their presence,
because to be honest,
their presence
has made all the difference
in the world.

And the messages
of hope and healing

they bring to you,
these are the messages
you gotta' believe in,
even when everything
inside of you
tells you otherwise,
tells you
they are wrong.

Let them be your eyes
when you cannot see for yourself.
Trust in their guidance.
And be grateful.
They were sent to you for a reason.

let go

Sometimes, it's hard to let go of the past. Some things you wish you could do over again, but know you'll never get an opportunity to do so.

You wish it could have been different; that things could have been different. There's so much you would have done differently, but for whatever reason, you just couldn't at the time. You weren't ready to.

And maybe that's the whole point. You're only ready for things, when you're ready for them– it's that simple.

Maybe that's what half of living is all about: accepting the things you weren't ready for, when you wish you were, when you so wish you had been.

And as for the other half of living?

Letting go of the idea that it could have been any different.

the light to shine through

Carl Jung once wrote,
"no tree, it is said, can grow to heaven
unless its roots reach down to hell."

And so, too, our roots must grow deep
down into hell, to be able
to reach up into heaven.

We must venture into the
deepest, darkest crevices of our being,
examine who we are in our essence, and only
then can we advance across to the other side,
and rise into happiness.

By facing the darkness, we
become the darkness, and when we
become the darkness we so fear,
we allow the light to shine through;
and in so doing, we become the light, too;

because all the darkness ever really wants,
is for the light to come shining through.

bleed eternal

And she said,
"may you always remember to pray
long and hard
for the things you need,
just as much as you do
for the things you want,
because what you want is all nice and good,
but what you need–
man, that stuff bleeds eternal."

***

The things we need and the things we want may not always be one in the same. May we all learn to differentiate the two, and to learn that what we want may be magnificent, but what we need is eternal.

The power of prayer lies in aligning yourself with the things you believe, deep inside, are best for your true purpose and calling. The stuff of prayer is real and difficult; it is not easy. And yet, it is vitally important–allowing you to be more conscious and aware of who you are meant to be, who you are called to be. May we all learn to pray not for the things we want, but for that which we need, and the courage to know the difference when it matters most, when the stakes are highest.

thankful

And what should you be most thankful for?

You should be most thankful for being alive, for being a living, breathing, sentient being on this earth; for being someone who is not afraid to feel the full spectrum of emotion bestowed upon us in this great mystery we call life. And not to fear these feelings, but to be patient and sit with them, to immerse yourself within them so that you may understand what it is they are trying to tell you. That is indeed rare in this day and age.

What a true gift that is.

There is great beauty in feeling the lows just as crisply and immersively as feeling the highs. The highs are high, and the lows are low–my God are they low.

But in all honesty, you need to feel it all–the highs and the lows. It's all part of it; it's all part of life. You cannot pick and choose. No one said it was ever going to be easy; these things rarely are. But it will definitely be worth it.

better days

Hope isn't always that bright, echoing call
piercing through the heavens.
It isn't always full of life and love,
of beauty.

Sometimes,
it's that broken,
fragmented
feeling
of
loneliness
filled with sweat and tears
urging you to keep going forward,
to keep moving onwards.

Not for the sake of today necessarily,
because today, life is ugly
and breathing, painful.

But for the sake of tomorrow,
for the hope that tomorrow
will be a better day.

Sometimes, hope is all we need
to move us forward.

stumble into love

To get a taste of heaven,
we must first experience hell.

To feel love,
we must first live through pain,
especially when the pain
is all we have left.

After all,
how else would we know
for certain
we've truly arrived
and stumbled into love?

the wars we wage

The greatest battles
you will ever have to face,
are the ones you wage
within yourself.

So grant yourself this one favor.
Let you,
win

safe // protected

Some dreams
are much too fragile for this world.
Some dreams,
it's best to keep inside,
tucked away,
safe and protected.
Like angel wings,
they effervesce
upon being exposed to the air.
The world
can be a harsh and unforgiving place.
It will take those dreams of yours,
and destroy them;
tell you they cannot be achieved,
tell you they are much too grand
for your little soul to dream upon.
That's why it's best
to keep some dreams, inside.
Safe and protected.

After all, what good is a dream
if the believer cannot believe in its magic?

potentiality

Sometimes, we paint people to be
who we want them to be.
We do not see them
for who they truly are.
Not all potential is (always) achieved,
and sometimes–
that's a good thing
& for the best.

the beauty in brokenness

When I was young, I tried to make it a personal goal to fix every broken relationship I had. It became a sort of game for me, to see how good I was at salvaging and repairing broken connections: things that no longer resembled what they once were.

Fragmented, torn-apart, and fragile vestibules of things once so sure of themselves.

But as I got older, I realized that some friendships cannot be mended. As hard as I tried, they just couldn't. The parts no longer fit the way they once did. They no longer made sense together. Call it growth or dysfunction, they just didn't connect.

I realized there is a sort of beauty and inevitability in the brokenness.

That maybe, certain people come into your life for a reason; and they leave once you have learned what it was they were meant to teach you in the first place.

And as for the ones that do stay:
those lessons, they last an entire lifetime…

the wallflower

The seedling undergoes
a sort of metamorphosis.
A rebirth into a sprout,
a vertical labyrinth
chiseling through the moist soil.
A soft nudge.
A quick trickle of fury.

It basks in the free-flow
of the brisk, morning air.
Suddenly, it is blinded by the rays of light,
as if a thousand suns
beckon for its growth towards infinity.
It begins to grow east, then south,
in a myriad of directions.

Without rhyme & without reason.

As it yields to the luminous voices of each sun,
the memories of its journey
are etched in knots
found along its lengthening stalk.
The stalk itself
a roadmap
of the journey the young sprout has traveled,
of where its come from.

With each promise of fortune and prosperity,
the stalk develops kinks and twists in its form.

No longer does it follow,
as it once did beneath the earth,
the straight path
in ultimate defiance of gravity.
If now wrestles with forces much greater,
with temptation and doubt.
with the dissonant nature of conflict.

And yet, the inner soul of the sapling
decrees its resolution
against the elements without.
And it knows,
all those twists and turns–it cannot forget.
But "what-is-to-come,"
it cannot deny either;
nor can it jeopardize...

Destiny smiles upon those who wander.

And so the sapling is blessed in its journey into
becoming a wallflower.

if

If you can make this experience your own.

If you can create beauty out of chaos,
meaning out of the ashes.

If you can sow the seeds of love
in the places of fear and hate within you,
and in time, stumble upon a thriving forest:

then don't you see,
you've already won.

the greatest source

Here is my wish for you–
may you come upon and find,
upon some distant day,
that all of your imperfections and losses,
those caustic tormentors of your soul,
have always been the source
of your greatest joys and triumphs.

***

Acceptance of the seemingly unacceptable
is the greatest form of grace we possess.

The transformation of suffering into
consciousness only occurs if you surrender to
the suffering.

Maybe it's in the acceptance of the imperfect,
that true perfection arises;
that we may attain it
once and for all.

I am a celebration

Who am I?

You are better off
asking the universe that question.
It can answer you far more accurately,
more eloquently,
than I ever can.

***

When I look in the mirror,
I see all the stars and galaxies
staring back at me.
Constellations of celebration.
A celestial choir singing a song in unison.
They are singing for me.
To me.

That is enough for any song
and any celebration.

the beauty of nowhere left

"There's nowhere left to look but inwards.
You'll find what you need there," he said.

"I don't know if I have anything left inside," she
replied.

"Oh you do," he said, "I've seen it…
and it's beautiful."

the storm, your mentor

The storm will pass.
This much I do know.
And in time,
you will find
you are blessed.
You always have been;

that the actions of others,
those whirlpools of heartache and desire
have very little to do with you.

The beauty resides within the suffering.
The light enters you in the broken places
and illuminates a depth of strength
within you
that you did not know you possessed,

that you've always possessed.

It teaches you.
It becomes your mentor.
During those sleepless nights
is when your perspective changes.
It's in those nights
when you find your meaning again;
your love for yourself,
who you were, and who you wish to be,
how you wish to love and be loved.

You learn it all again.
All over again.

To be appreciated,
just as a flower is admired
without being plucked
from it's divine source.
And so too will you believe again.
Believe that life is love,
and pain is love longing for compassion,
waiting to be set free.
All of divinity exists within you.

And it takes those tears
to feel that love again.
It takes those fears
to make you whole again.
And then one day, you'll realize.
The storm has passed,
the sun has risen,
and the skies in the horizon
have already long-forgotten
what once ruptured their calm,
peaceful silence.

fallen angels

Some angels come into your life
because they need your help.
They've fallen.
Their gossamer wings
are much too fragile for this world.

So when you witness a fallen angel,
don't turn away.
Don't be afraid.
Help to mend her wings,
and her broken spirit.
There is beauty
in seeing this through.

See to it
that she shines once more,
that she believes once again
in who she is,
in the beauty of life,
in the goodness of the human heart.

Because if she doesn't, then who will?

soulful wishes

And her final wish for me:
"may you always have an abundance
of all the things
that feed your soul,
and less of those
which feed your ego."

***

May we learn to appreciate the distinction
between the things that feed our ego,
and those that feed our soul.

for nene 2.0

A photograph.
It was a simple photograph.
I even had it printed because I liked it so much.

The photograph is of my grandmother and me,
our heads in juxtaposition, cheek-touching-
cheek, our heads cradled by the soft down pillow
of her nursing home bed. Her soft droopy
eyelids are clasped shut, her once-defined
cheekbones dulled by the fates of old age.

She is asleep. She looks serene.

The contagious smile she wore so frequently
caused only a limited wrinkling of her skin.
Truth be told, she looked much younger than she
really was. Time had been kind to her
complexion.

My eyes are then drawn to myself in the photo.
I'm leaning-in close to her, as close as the
uncomfortable aluminum chair adjacent to her
bed may permit. My spine is arched, my frame
at an angle.

Why do I love this picture so much?

Perhaps it reminds me of a certain quiescence
that sleep offers–a type of serenity built into the

very fabric of our being, and programmed into our circadian rhythm; I imagine the serenity of sleep was very welcoming to my grandmother, because when she is asleep, I know that the whims of a volatile disease known as Alzheimer's cannot torment her any longer. Her ceaseless fears of losing herself over and again, have vanished. She is found.

She is at peace.

As am I.

In that photo, we are content.

I swear we are infinite.

Another reason for my affection towards this photograph is that it helps me remember one of the many truths my grandmother had taught me over the years: that in the end, death is eternal sleep. And all the contriving, fashioning and fathoming we do to build our fortresses of wealth, fame, and fortune–all of those things, mean nothing, in the end. We cannot take any of them with us, perchance only memories of such extravagance.

But maybe the most important reason why I love this photograph so much, is because of the simple fact that I know when my grandmother is asleep, she is being greeted by God's angels. They are singing in unison, a choir from the Heavens. A song of festivity–a testament to the kind, giving, nurturing life she once had and continues to possess.

Their gentle song is the stuff of celebration for the children, grandchildren, and great-grandchildren she has helped raise, and the values she has instilled within their hearts, never to be overcome by the ravaging breakers of life's implacable oceans.

Their song is a celebration of a life that will not end by death and mortal decay, but rather will live on, in the stories that we will share of her animating and enduring spirit. Accounts of how she has touched our lives, and even of strangers' lives every time she invited the poor into her home to feed and clothe, and every time she left a bowl of warm milk out in the backyard for the neighborhood cats to congregate and hold vigil overnight–with the flickering aura of the lampposts above serving as candlelight.

They are the stories of her enduring faith; lessons of a complete trust in a loving God who never gave you more than you could handle, but always enough to make you grow. I often remember our conversations, almost always pertained to me: my joys, my struggles, my passions. She was rarely interested in talking about herself; always consumed with others.

"How are you, grandma?" I would ask.

And with a smile, she would reply, "Let's not talk about me; how are you doing? How was school today?"

She gave to others that gift of empathy and understanding which seems so scarce in this world today–the precious presence of a human being who would listen and comfort another because the person before her mattered.

He or she was a sister, a brother, a loved one, a friend.

And to do any less would be to nullify the sacred bond we all share as human beings inhabiting this earth, together and united. She lived out her faith and spread goodness in the ways she knew how, so that this world may be a better place when she leaves it, than it may have been had she never been born.

I imagine when the final day comes, Heaven will be kind to my grandmother, for she was kind to it and all its creation.

A choir of angels will lift her to the home to

which she was born to return; I bet it would be as breathtaking as witnessing the first Dawn on earth. Arising in a dense forest. The only sounds perhaps coming from the initial rustling of activity among the indigenous population of creatures on an island no eye has seen, unperturbed by man's grandiose imaginings, for she herself knew that existence should not be defined, nor measured by symbols of indulgence.

Instead, true beauty is to be found simply by virtue of being alive, and having that opportunity to spread goodness–

wherever it may go,
wherever it is needed,
and to whomever it may reach.

Dawn is the perfect word to illustrate the time of day my grandmother will be greeted by the Holy Ghost.

After-all, she was given that name for a reason...

I miss you, Nene.

complications within the gray

Guilt and regret are two emotions so delicately-intertwined with one another, that one can hardly begin delineate where one ends and the other begins.

Neither emotion feels particularly good to the human experience. Your stomach revolves in sequential knots, you feel an immense darkness clouding your mind, and delicate muscles, ones you never once suspected of existing, begin pulling and gnawing along your face, forming wrinkly-contortions whereupon your own reflection in a mirror may seem unrecognizable. Both emotions are known to express such symptoms.

But how do you make the pain stop?

Is there a foolproof method to tame the beast, and be free from its grip?

Only once was I offered a remedy worth remembering, and it came in the form of the following story, by virtue of a dear friend's struggle with her own personal demon, and her subsequent revelation about the significance of its power.

Here's her story…

***

"Okay Miss, that's the end of our procedure."

She stared across the cold, white-washed
linoleum floor; her eyes froze upon a painting of
the Grand Canyon adorning the wall ahead. She
noticed the sunset in the evening sky
illuminating the gargantuan, jagged dips of rock,
like a spotlight upon a stage.

And she felt at the center of that stage.

"Excuse me, Miss Chisom? You're all done,"
the concerned physician repeated. "Are
you feeling okay? You'll be happy to know the
procedure was a great success. I'll lead you to
my secretary's desk, where we can schedule
your follow-up."

He extended his hand.

"Oh I'm sorry, I don't know what got into me!
Thank you doctor," she replied.

And as she grasped his thick sweaty palm, she
used its weight to maneuver herself out of the
oddly-shaped machine to which she was secured

during the episode.

***

The entire ordeal commenced a few months prior, when she had met this marketing firm executive while on vacation in New York City. What was only supposed to be a few martini's at a happy hour turned into a bi-coastal romance. They engaged in telephone conversations, video calls and took full advantage of all social media platforms; they even made an informal pact to visit one another every few weeks in an alternating fashion.

She was to fly to New York City, and he to Los Angeles.

Gradually, Dido grew tired of the frenzy of travel. And at the refusal of either party to relocate, they split rather amicably. The only real dilemma they needed to address was the 2-month-old life-form developing within Dido's uterus.

She recognized the ambiguity of her fate–how it lay claim to a world of judgment many would describe as the 'gray zone.' She had witnessed political pundits and social activists alike argue the issues for and against the practice of abortion. She read extensively about the variances in conviction between the sanctity of life and personal autonomy:

Does a woman's right to choose outweigh the sacredness of life? Or does this sacred nature undermine the personal freedoms to which a woman is entitled? And of course, there is even debate as to when exactly an embryo can be referred to as living–and if that sort of attention to minutiae should even matter?

And so in accordance with her former suitor and girlfriends' fairly-explicit sentiments, and in resonance with her most conscious of beliefs, she carried through with the abortion.

No one, however, herself included, could have predicted the degree of depression to which she would succumb after the procedure. Regret loaded upon her the weight of the entire biosphere, and her shoulders were much too weak.

They failed her.

What was she to do with her guilt?

The emotion itself resembled a heavy

hammer beating down upon her tender, tired heart. At the age of 23, she was so young to have faced such a struggle.

Did she make the right decision? How would she know that? If she did, why did she feel so sad?

But then it dawned upon her: the idea expressed itself like a breeze through her own lips during one of her weekly psychotherapy sessions.

Dr. Zigg asked her, "so Dido, it seems you've tried to release your guilt, to mitigate the pain, by empathizing with yourself. You've tried to be more understanding of your prior situation and how you didn't know any better. And yet, you've still not been able to find forgiveness. Why do you think that is so?"

Dido hesitated for a moment and reflected upon her therapist's inquiry. A gentle grin attached itself to her lips, a subconscious attempt to minimize the tightening of wrinkles on the corners of her mouth.

And she replied:

"Maybe I don't want to forget about it!" she exclaimed. "I don't want to wipe this memory clean. My guilt is an ever-present reminder–if

life finds me in a similar future
circumstance, not to repeat the same judgment."

She paused a moment, enough to notice the
silence synchronously broken only by the
arbitrary movement of the clock on the corner
shelf.

The timepiece had no method of judging the
episode in progress. But the therapist was not
blind to the insights currently being expressed.
And neither was Dido; so she continued.

"It's almost like a memento or souvenir I carry
from a land visited in the past. In my opinion, it
takes a truly courageous and empathetic person
to exist with these feelings, and understand their
importance."

"The guilt I feel has a function. It serves a
purpose of greater significance to my
innermost being if I remember it, than merely
brush this whole incident aside and forget it ever
occurred."

"Don't get me wrong! I'm not beating myself up
over this. I acknowledge that it was the best
decision I could have made at the time with what
I knew; it was the most I knew back then, and so
it was the best choice I could have made. But I
still don't want to forget it ever occurred...I

mean how can I?! Not for a second! Our culture really demonizes guilt and makes us believe it's unhealthy. Society offers ample instruction on ways to make it disappear; it makes us believe the only good feeling is the one that feels good."

"But just because it doesn't feel good, doesn't mean it isn't important."

"It's a really powerful emotion, guilt is. It may feel nasty when projected to the past and you find yourself incessantly dwelling upon your mistakes and errors in judgment. But projected towards the future, this same regret empowers me to change and improve: to be a better person today, than who I was yesterday."

"And to be honest, I can barely recognize the woman I was back then. We need to listen more to our emotions. They are our guides especially in our complications within the gray: they rarely lie."

And just like that, their time was up.

a song of courage

"*N*?"

"No. come on, I know you know this."

"*O*?"

"No….try again. you'll get it this time."

"*R*?"

"No, what comes after *K*, Jonathan. *H*, *I*, *J*, *K*…?"

"*T*!!"

***

I've had numerous volunteer experiences during my high school years, but none of them can compare in meaning to my experience at the Salvation Army.

"America's best kept secret," they say.

Indeed, I found out for myself that every bit of that cryptic proclamation is true.

I must have passed that old building in my hometown numerous times, never knowing what lurked behind those tall, arcane, cemented barricades. It almost seemed like they wanted to keep what was inside, protected–as if what lay beyond was some sort of untold fortune. Little did I know that there did exist a treasure of sorts, for it turns out I discovered one of my passions within those walls–tutoring grade school children in an after-school program. Truth be told, however, they taught me so much more than I could have ever hoped to teach them.

One particular story about a child whom I taught, comes to mind. And it behooves the reader to understand the following preface:

Jonathan is in the 3rd grade; he does not know his *ABC*'s.

***

Often, the children were given a word assignment consisting of reorganizing a given list of 20 words in alphabetical order. Needless to say, during the ensuing weeks, the set of words became more complex, with each word often beginning with identical letters down to the third or fourth character.

Most of the kids excelled in this linguistic

exercise, except for Jonathan, because of the aforementioned reason.

We would rehearse the alphabet together dozens of times. I would request that he write the letters down on a sheet of paper prior to commencing the exercise, usually on the upper right-hand margin. And he would almost invariably be stumped at the third or fourth spot along the continuum of letters, resulting in the creation of a word list of seemingly non-cohesive parts out of a complete sum.

Weeks of little-to-no progress turned to months of stalemate–for the exercises only became more involved, and Jonathan was barely able to consolidate the minute gains he had made the week prior.

Then I acquired my revelation! I could not explain where it came from–rather I was more flustered as to why I had not thought of it sooner.

I called over two of the other children; passed on the instruction. We all took a brief pause, and in unison began reciting to Jonathan the song that has graced classrooms all across the world since (it seems) the dawn of human literacy–the *ABC*'s.

After a few renditions of the tune, Jonathan learned the song and sang it to us, and to himself.

The term 'joy' is not sufficient enough to describe the emotion of intense elation he felt as he pitched the final measures of the harmony. Two things happened that day: the stock market rose a few extra points by the evening's close, and no one ever laughed at Jonathan again for not knowing his *ABC*'s.

"You know, it's a miracle that you were able to learn this much of the alphabet without the song, don't you?" I remarked.

"Yea I guess," he answered slyly as his two front teeth poked through a grin.

***

Courage.

Courage is a quality that is not only found in the hearts of soldiers who run into an opposing blaze of artillery fire. Nor is it exclusively possessed by the spirit of firefighters who risk their lives to save people they've never met, lest be engulfed by violent, torrential flames.

It has also built a home within the quiet, resilient souls of children just like Jonathan, who spirit through day to day, performing poorly in school because they were never taught a simple lesson that may have made all the difference, that would have made all the difference–an answer to their long, perceived struggle. And so they return and try once more the very next day.

Courage is present in the moment we fall, and pick ourselves back up, not necessarily because anyone believes in us, but because we believe in ourselves: because we dream to achieve a greatness not confined to any preconceived, set-standard of the term found within a classroom, or in a meeting room. Rather, this excellence we exuberate in our sense of being; it permeates the very fabric of our existence–a brilliance of being present that on some fundamental level, we feel we owe to ourselves.

It's just that we lose this feeling when we grow older. This deep-rooted desire seems to effervesce somewhere in the piercing spectrum of responsibility bestowed upon us by a world that we don't entirely understand, and which so often doesn't foster the fulfillment of our true inner needs by way of deception and false promises.

But this flame of destiny need not disappear. It

may remain in our psyche, much like a melody would. The only real task that remains is to break down those stone barricades we've built for ourselves, so that our melodies can flow forth, freely and without shame…

wings to fly

Sometimes, we forget
we were born with wings,
for the struggles
we so ache
to crawl through,
we were really always meant
to fly through.

odds & promises

Promise me,
you'll never stop dreaming.
Not when things are well;
but rather when you feel the odds
stacked against you.

Promise me,
that you will imagine your success
long before you've achieved it.
And feel those feelings associated
with that triumph,
long before it is called to be yours.

Promise me,
in those moments of adversity,
you will rediscover the light within you,
that wellspring of gratitude,
that has laid dormant and forgotten,
waiting to be reignited
upon even the faintest of a spark.

the stillness of growth

You may not see it now,
but these quiet years in your life,
these moments of lethargy and stagnation,
of quiet desperation,
where nothing seems to be happening
or going your way,
are just as important
as those periods of noticeable growth.

Perhaps even more so.

It's during these moments of stillness
that something is growing within you,
taking shape, holding form,
palpating to its edges.
Your edges.

Be patient in the midst of this growth.

***

Some periods of your life are meant for
transformation. They are transitional periods,
where you assess and reassess your values and
perspectives subconsciously; the most important
of which relate to how you see yourself and how
you feel you impact others around you.

Be patient with all the work occurring deep
within you, and be kind to the person that life is
allowing to emerge slowly from within.

So take your time and grow.
Mature.
So you may thrive.

remember to remember

You've got to believe
wholeheartedly
on some fundamental, elemental level,
that everything you've ever left behind
pales in comparison
to everything that's in store for you,
that life is going to bring your way.
And that can be an especially hard thing to do,
when you don't have the answers,
when you seem lost and confused,
when the stars don't seem to be aligning for you,
when you're in the
'in-betweens' of life,
done with the past
but not quite 'there-yet' in the future.
But maybe that's when
you need to believe it the most
during those transitional periods:
to have faith in that
is everything
during those vulnerable moments.

Remember
to remember that.

ON GRACE & FORGIVENESS

forgiveness

Perhaps forgiveness
is when you no longer have any ill-will,
any feeling of malice,
towards the person who has harmed you;
not because they don't deserve it,
but because you know
full-well
what real suffering feels like,
and you don't wish that
upon any human being.

the bend of the wildflower

If we are to be like wildflowers,
bending our bodies
to seal and steal away
the sunlight from another,
then maybe forgiveness
is the realization
that the sunshine is found
all around us.

the fantasy of the past

The past
must remain
in the past,
for your present self
to claim it's future.

***

Every now and then,
don't be afraid
to change your story,
your narrative.

Because with every change,
every bend and break,
you are shedding the parts of you,
you thought you so desperately needed,
but now realize were superficial,
disposable falsehoods,
adopted to please others.

They were never the real you,
but fragments of fantasy
you thought you needed to be,
to be faithful to others.

But life is calling you

to be faithful
to your rightful self.

forgive yourself

You need to forgive yourself
just as much as you need to forgive others.

Forgive yourself for all the times
you sold yourself short.

For all the times
you failed to grasp your true worth.

For all the times
you allowed others to treat you unkindly.

For all the times you did the best you could,
with what you knew and what you were given,
at the time.

For all the sunsets you failed to appreciate,
and all the sunrises you thought would never
come.

For all the times you wished upon a star
and doubted the reciprocity of the universe.

For all the times you ceased to believe
in a loving creator
who has the entire world
rigged in your favor.

Forgiveness is the highest form of love–

and this, above all else,
you owe to yourself.

permission to rise

Does the sun ask the earth
for permission to rise?

Does the moon ask the stars
for permission to incandesce the night sky?

Then why must you beg another
for permission to forgive?

Why must you wait for another's apology,
to heal and let go?

If the entire universe
can bear the suffering of all its inhabitants
with dignity and grace,
and if you are the entire universe,
in eternal motion,
reborn and aware of itself,
over and again,
what have you got to fear?

And what have you got to lose?

the greatest gift

The greatest give I've ever received wasn't offered to me by another. It was never placed snugly beneath a Christmas tree, ordained in shiny paper wrapping. It was, rather, something I found within myself, discovered purely by happenstance.

I was never aware I possessed this gift, for I was never before in the right circumstance or frame of mind to accept it–truly to appreciate it. The gift took all those years of living to materialize, all of those sacrifices of learning, trials and tribulations. They were necessary for the evolution of its embodiment; a process that as mentioned before, required effort and failure. Much like a growing oak lunges its roots deep into the earth, and hopes to permeate the many layers of dense soil for its foundation and wellspring of nutrition, I too underwent a similar transformation. Except mine did not seem, during its course, to be as meticulously planned as that found in nature's design, but in retrospect I now see that perhaps it was.

The gift about which I write is the intention and the act of forgiveness. It is first and foremost an intention; an inner conviction or a sort of promise to yourself. It is also an act; nothing is possible by simple will. One must will to do, and then to act in order to attain the end to which he is destined.

Our journeys vary, and so do our respective receptivities and collective willingness to comprehend the answers that nature provides. They are ubiquitous by design. It is no coincidence that every year, migratory birds sear through the ether, with an unparalleled sense of proprioception, to head south for the winter. In touch with the earth's magnetic forces, they are one with the dynamism found all around them. Such events occur readily throughout the animal kingdom. Nature calls, and the animals listen. They do not talk, they listen. Perhaps we should heed the call as well.

And so, I began to listen to the signs all around me. And what I discovered was the greatest gift I've ever received:

that the aim of forgiveness is not to change the past, but rather to change the present by altering one's view of the past–to see the past through a different lens, as it were.

I've discovered that this feat of courage cannot be attained without the comprehension and compassion that empathy may bestow: empathy for the other, and empathy for yourself.

To forgive does not condone a transgression; rather it lifts the muddy veil of hatred and indignation superficially held over another and within yourself, so that he can be viewed as who he really is–an imperfect human being. And you can be viewed for who you are–also an imperfect human being.

And it is only through empathy, that one can understand the motives and feelings of the other, which spurred the transgression that came to pass. When you witness a crippled soul, flailing at others and causing harm, insecure about his own significance in the world; when you see the inner terror that pervades his soul, his weakness and fear of others, and ultimately, his fear of death, you cannot help but forgive.

It is all you can do for another; the best gift you can grant for yourself–for you too would want the same done for you.

how do I forgive?

Tell me,
how do I forgive?
Teach me.
I'm here to listen.
I am all yours.

Show me how to forgive those things, which
seem so impossible to. Give me the strength, the
courage, to let go of things not meant for me, but
seem so integral to my existence right now. I
cannot even tell the difference anymore between
what I'm meant to carry, and what I'm not. Help
me know that difference.

My burdens are heavy; I was never meant to
carry such things.

the (un)forgivable(s)

Forgiveness of the seemingly unforgiveable is the greatest form of grace we possess on this earth. It is the ultimate form of self-love: to free yourself of everything you fear to lose, so you may attain everything that is meant for you. It does not condone what happened, but rather, releases the heaviness and allows you the freedom to move forward with a pure heart, and an enduring spirit.

ON HEALING & GROWTH

a phoenix

A *phoenix* only rises
when she recognizes
that the ashes below
are her own.

shedding away (to become who we are)

In order to grow, you need to be willing to let go of the things that no longer serve you. You need to be aware of them, identify them, and be willing to lose them. Without guilt, without shame, without judgment, for they once were important parts of you with which you identified. And had you not lived further, you would not have arrived at the realization that you no longer needed them–for they no longer have anything to offer you. And so, it is through this ever-evolving process that we grow, shedding away parts of ourselves we no longer need, so that we may rise…

the space between

The space that exists,
between 'no longer' and 'not yet,'
is sacred;
and the art of living,
lies in showing that space
patience and compassion
as often as you can,
and as much as you can.

***

The greatest act we can allow ourselves to do is
to treat the space between 'no longer' and 'not
yet' with kindness and love.

Allow yourself to visit that place often, without
judgment.

Sit with it, and be present.

Be kind, and allow yourself to evolve in the way
in which you were meant to evolve, into the
person you were meant to be, without resistance,
and with love. Be patient with all the growth
taking place within you. And know that life is
always in the right.

this moment is everything

Maybe everything there ever was
and everything there ever will be,
lies in this moment.

All the ghosts of yesterday,
the souls of tomorrow,
convene here
together
with us.

Bearing witness
to who we are.

And reminding us,
that everything
we wish we were
is still attainable.

***

So often, we tend to live our lives either lost in
past memories, wishing we can redo or relive an
experience, or we look ahead into the future,
hoping we will finally arrive to where we are
meant to be.

But maybe, the present moment is all there ever really is, and in embracing the present, we allow ourselves to be ready to accept what we are destined to receive next–

without worry, without judgment, fully present.

parts of you

Maybe everything you are,
you've scattered around
in the people and places
you've met along the way...

And when you meet
that person or place again,
you recognize the parts within you,
left behind forever in them.

***

We become one another's reflections, staring
back at each other. So like a pair of eyes
becoming conscious of itself in another pair of
eyes, we exist beyond infinity, beyond space and
time. There is beauty in this existence.

gifts of healing

Maybe we finally heal,
when we are able to give to others,
those things we never received,
ourselves.

And in so doing, we receive them too.

***

Learning to heal involves giving to others the
parts of you, that you feel were denied.

heal the darkness

You heal the darkness
within you, by shining
your light into the very same darkness
found within someone else.

phases & deep breathing

Most of us believe
that life consists
of one single breath.
Constant, never changing.

But in reality,
life arrives to us in phases.
Each phase necessary
for the next to occur.

And so,
like successive segments of a tree trunk,
each completing its circular orbit
to greet its complementary sibling
on the other side,
our life is created as such.

And at any given moment,
the phase found within me
greets its complimentary phase
found within you.

And in so doing, we rejoice.

your right to bloom

You've got to bloom
in all the places
and in all the ways
they never thought you would–

not to prove them wrong,
but to prove yourself right.

to flourish, within & without

I don't want simply to live.
I want to flourish.
I want to thrive.
To feel one with the moon and the stars,
the heavens above and below,
within and without,
to be wholly conscious
that I belong to infinity.
Nothing more, and nothing less.

Isn't that the whole damn point of living?

embers of pride

But most of all,
be proud,
and rejoice in the fact
that after all of this,
you still believe
in the goodness of the human heart
and the resilience of the human spirit.

That you can still believe
in the smiles and laughter of children,
and know they aren't for naught.

That you can still exude to others,
stories of the many blessings
bestowed upon your life,
in all the shapes and forms
by which they are delivered–
as wrapped gifts of love or pain,
devotion or betrayal,
and still be grateful.

You are a shining light
in a world encapsulated by fear and hate,
radiating your burning embers of love,
without condition,
without circumstance.

You just do, because you just are.
And that's what you should be most proud of.

the beautiful everglow

It's not mean to be difficult;
it's meant to be simple.
All beautiful things are.

Like a breath of air,
the warm touch of the everglow,
the purity of our souls,
just are.

wishing upon a shooting star

All the shooting stars
I've ever wished upon
have all led me back to myself,
reminding me
to believe in the power of
my destiny.

lessons of consciousness

The universe gives and takes away,
based on what has served its purpose
in our lives.

When we have fully-learned a lesson
we were meant to learn,
the universe pulls us
out of a particular circumstance
and offers a new one in its place
for us to master.

And in this way,
we become more and more conscious
of the entire universe within us.

We are, in our deepest essence,
the entire universe in motion,
becoming conscious of itself.

the carryings of change

Much has changed since last I visited here.
The memories I made seem more distant now
than they did years before,
and yet strangely familiar.

It was here where I forged
some of my strongest bonds with others,
and with myself.

So where do I go from here?

I take comfort in knowing that there is beauty in
the distance between where you left off and
where you are: where you've come from, and
where you've travelled. And it's up to you, it is
your responsibility, to embrace the sometimes
fleeting circumstances that have brought you
here, to own them, and to create for yourself a
new life from this moment forward.

The beauty lies in knowing that nothing stays
the same, and living anyway. It lies in realizing
that things will change, and believing anyway:
believing in the moments that have propelled
you here, and the moments that will carry you
away from here.

Ever beautiful, ever changing.

this new year's fire

Here's to everything
you wish you were
this past year.

Your fires within,
your meaning without,
your purpose in plain site.

All of it,
defined,
materialized,
born,
in this new year.

the rebuild 1.0

Some years are meant
for rebuilding.
Some years are destined
to be 'game-changers:' years
that mold you
into the person you are called to be.

Some years are to be grasped
head-on, held onto,
and worked the hell out of,
in order for your dreams to emerge,
and your demons to die.

May next year
be such a year
for us all.

freedom in the gray

Light cannot exist
without darkness;
each exists within the other.

***

So often, we tend to believe that everything we
experience can be categorized as either "good"
or "bad." But in reality, the positive & negative
forces in our lives are much more
complementary, more interconnected, than we
often envision them to be. These seemingly
opposite entities are really interdependent, and
create a sort of harmony and balance within life.

One flows from the other, so that you no longer
are aware of where one ends, and the other
begins.

Most things that are important are not black or
white. They are not right or wrong. And it's in
the gray unknown where you discover your true
humanity: your freedom to choose how you wish
to respond and what to take responsibility for.
The thoughts you wish to entertain and those of
which you choose to let go. The struggles you
rise above only after having learned the meaning

of loss. Because at the end of the day, all you may have left is the peace found within the four corners of your mind, and the love present within the four chambers of your heart.

And if you're lucky, if you're truly lucky, you just may find both.

the rebuild 2.0

Some years are meant
for rebuilding
who you thought
you were,
only to discover
that you
never needed to build anything,
at all.

Everything you wish you were,
you already are.
You possess your entire destiny
in the palm of your hand.

so much greater

And my grandfather said,
"try not to place your worth
in anything or anyone,
in any loss or failure,
victory or triumph.

Place it within yourself.
You are so much greater
than the sum of your experiences;
so much incredibly greater
than anything and everything
that's ever happened to you.

Does the sun need to exclaim to the heavens
how brilliant and powerful she is?
No, she just shines,
without explanation, without apology,
pure and simple.
And so, too, should you.
The light found within you,
let it shine through."

inhale // exhale

Exhale the old,
inhale the new;
because some breaths,
you were never meant to hold onto,
anyway.

revelations

We reveal to others
how they should treat us,
by how we treat ourselves.

So just as the waves
wash upon the shoreline,
to remind the earth
just how beautiful the ocean really is,
be sure to remind yourself
just how worthy you are.

underdogs

Sometimes,
underdogs
become
topdogs.

***

Never count the underdog out. It is exactly during these moments of doubt and uncertainty, when everyone has counted him out, that he thrives. He is able to consolidate his inner strength, garner all the faith he holds dear to his heart, and overcome adversity.

It is precisely in these moments, and because of them, that he thrives and perseveres. He can bear any 'how,' any 'why,' any circumstance, any obstacle that comes his way.

He cannot be stopped, for his meaning lies within.

the struggle to leave behind

The struggle is,
always has been,
and always will be,

to let go of the things
that no longer serve you,
and to embrace all the goodness
waiting for you.

Especially in the moments
when you may not see it...

not just yet.

Because everything
you have to look forward to,
is so far better
than anything and everything
you've ever left behind.

wins & losses

No wins & no losses.
No beginning & no end.
Each moment is present
for the next to unfold.
And everything is
as it is meant to be.

angel wings

Angels are not born;
they learn to grow their wings with time.
They are difficult to see
because upon achieving awareness
of what truly matters and what doesn't,
they no longer choose to stay grounded.

Rather, they hover
in the infinite spaces
amidst the crowds,
watching and laughing
at those devoting their entire lives
to things without meaning–
things that bring no joy or love to their lives.

The material.

For they know
what truly matters
is the love you give to another,
and the warmth he or she feels
when being surrounded
by angel wings.

souls & stardust

Sometimes, all you need
is a simple nod from the universe.
An acknowledgment
that some of the greatest beauty in life
arises from the 'not-knowing.'

And as you peel back the layers,
you realize that the mystery found "out-there"
is ultimately the mystery found within you.

And with every step in the journey,
life is revealing to you,
different layers of that mystery,
the mystery of who we all truly are,
souls draped in stardust...

love is enough

Perhaps the greatest gift
is to know that we are loved,
and that we are enough,
just as we are.
No amount of guilt and shame,
betrayal and loss,
can ever change that.
In fact, it is because of those things,
and not in spite of them,
that we are enough.
And we are loved.

We are enough.
We have always been enough.

the search, the grind, the struggle

The answers you seek
to the questions you ask
lie within the search.
They are the search.

***

The answers rarely come
without the struggle,
without the grinding
toil and strife;
because the struggle
is what you need,
to make sense of the answers.

Otherwise, you wouldn't understand,
let alone recognize them,
had they presented themselves to you
any sooner.

The struggle is what gives the answers
any sort of meaning to you.

beautiful, in time

Some things
aren't meant to be understood,
or examined.

They are to be appreciated;
in time, they become beautiful.

for // to

And this much
I know to be true:
that life is always happening
for us and not to us.

our freedom, our destiny

We create our own destiny–
our freedom to choose
who we are
and how we wish to respond
in any given situation.

No matter the circumstance,
we are always free to decide
who we wish to be
and how we choose to act.

And that freedom,
no one can take away from us.

some stories

Some stories,
you need to replace
with new ones; not
because they weren't true,
but because
they no longer serve you.

May all the stories
we tell ourselves
in the quiet recesses of our minds,
be kind and loving.

And may we have the courage
to let go of the ones
that no longer serve us.

The past has already been written;
but the future has yet to be so.

the paths of wonder

To live in wonder
is to stray from the path you're on,
and know
full-well,
that the new path you've chosen
is still a part of the old.
They are the same path
and lead to the same destination.

***

Your experiences are meant for you
and only you,
because believe me,
life is always in the right.

crossroads of character

Every once in a while,
you are faced with a decision:
a crossroads of sorts.

And at this juncture,
you have the opportunity
to make the choice
that will preserve your dignity.
And build your character.

I pray, time and again,
that you make that choice.
I pray that you find it
within your awareness
to search for and recognize
these hidden opportunities for that choice–
these special moments to create yourself
and recreate yourself, constantly.

Just as the moon wills her phases to be,
so too, I hope, will you.

be here now

Be here now. I pray.
Be in this moment, ever present.

Believe me,
you will have plenty of opportunities
to live in the future when it arrives.

And God only knows
how often you will relive your past.

But for now: just be.

Be you.

Be here.

Ever present.

Now.

work in progress

Learn to love yourself forever as a work in progress. There is no final destination because all there ever really is, is to be found in this moment. Be present in the stillness of you who are. Allow yourself to feel the echoes of all of eternity, of times long-passed and times yet to occur, reverberating within your rib cage. Your heart beats at the same tempo as that with which the stars quiver. And know that you are already perfect.

borne

All decision, and indecision
is borne of either love,
or fear.
It's that simple, really.

finding healing

May you find healing
in the places you least expect,
and because of the places
you least expect.

***

Healing isn't always an active, linear process.
Sometimes, it takes place gradually over time,
amidst the most unlikely of circumstances. The
most we can do is to create an environment of
acceptance–to allow the seemingly
unforgiveable, to be forgiven.

multiple lifetimes

At least a few times in life,
you need to reinvent yourself.
Over and over, time and again,
and in effect, you end up living
multiple lifetimes.

With each lifetime
existing within the other
as faint memories,
or bits of a dream
quietly revealing itself to you while you
slumber;
reminding you of where you've come from.

their own why

The greatest works of art
arise out of a necessity to create–
to express a feeling, a thought, a desire–
with a sort of honesty
and transparency
that cannot be articulated in any other way.

They are not borne of an insecure yearning
for approval or praise,
but rather,
stand alone upon pillars of belonging.
They belong to all of eternity.

They are at their essence vulnerable,
yet they flourish;
they do so inherently.
Naturally.

They are their own purpose;
their own "why."

the reassurance of the artist

Art is, at it's best, a vulnerable expression of a feeling, thought, or experience. No single piece of art is better than another. It just is. It exists. And is pure.

The trouble is, some artists constantly seek reassurance from others.

Is my art any good?

Do you like it?

They are seeking reassurance from the outside, when they should be looking for it from within.

It's comparable to a small boat floating in a vast ocean, being tossed around by the waverings of opinion. Just as there are a myriad waves, so too are there opinions.

Ask yourself.

Did I need to write this?

Was it worthwhile?

Does it add greater meaning to the world and make it into a better place?

May it inspire another soul to find meaning in a world at times so seemingly devoid of it?

The opinion that matters most is your own. And that transformation from seeking reassurance from outside yourself to within yourself is a beautiful thing.

the world of the artist

All artists long for a world they don't see,
that they hope is there;
that it exists.
It's not so much they hate the world
they're living in,
rather they just know
there is a better world out there,
waiting to be grasped
with their warm fingertips.
They hope this world to be true & real & good,
where love and pain are two sides
of the same coin,
and are transferable
from person and person,
much as a flower would be
when gifted to another.
It's a world in which the pain you feel,
you know, is really someone else's pain too;
and your love, theirs to share also–
that the energy you possess never dies,
but is rooted and reborn in the people and places
you've met along the way.
In this way, in this world,
it is all connected.

We are all connected.
We are all one.

the journey, an evolution

Learning to love
the distances in between
is sometimes
the most beautiful thing
we can allow ourselves to do.

***

It's a foreign concept really,
because we tend to think
about people, places, and things
in terms of the definite.

But everything changes,
people and places rarely stay the same.
And to appreciate the change,
we may look to respect the distances
that people have traveled, to be who they are.
And that means allowing ourselves
to feel kindness and love
for the distances we ourselves have traveled,
and have yet to travel.

There is beauty in the journey;
and gratitude in the evolution.

meaning in darkness

To create meaning
out of darkness,
love out of chaos:
these are what life
asks of us.

nothing lasts forever

Nothing lasts forever.

So if you find yourself in love,
indulge in it
and don't take it for granted.

And if you find yourself in pain,
don't be afraid to feel it through,
and learn the lessons you were meant to learn.

Destiny is calling.
Because nothing lasts forever.
And that's what makes it so sweet.

head & heart

Because everything you see,
you really experience twice–
once with your eyes,
and once with your mind's eye.

eternal empires

And she said, "I hope the empire you are building, is made less of brick and mortar, bank accounts and liquid assets; and more of the stuff of laughter and embraces, family and hope. Because the latter, stay with you forever."

the magic in lessons of gold

There is such a thing as outgrowing the past. When you no longer have a need or desire to revisit an experience, a person, or a place, because you've realized that it no longer serves a purpose in your life. That you've taken your lessons of gold, those pearls of wisdom, buried them within you, and internalized their meaning–so that you don't even know where you end, and the lessons begin. You both become one.

What a magical thing that is...

to attract the truth

May it be known,
at any given moment,
we attract exactly
what we need.

Nothing more
and nothing less.

***

May it be known, that we attract just what we
need, exactly when we need it the most. Life
often sends us the lessons we need to learn by
way of the people we meet, and the situations in
which we find ourselves. It's in how we respond
to these circumstances, that our true character is
built. Our true selves emerge once we take
advantage of all that life has to offer, and all it
has to teach us.

the mother robin

There he perched, majestically atop one of the branches of the tallest oak tree in the park; he was calm, at peace with what he had done.

A black bird of death.

A gentle breeze rustled through his cold feathers and the foliage. And she, sitting at a park bench far below, was watching the scene take place. Letting it all soak in.

Suddenly, she witnessed a small robin, the size of roughly her clenched fist or her beating heart, screeching angrily through the quiet. The innocent bird leapt into the air, glided through the wind, and repeatedly struck at the other bird–a hawk.

This ferocious predator had obliterated one of her babies. It was all instinct really; he was not to blame. But the mother robin was also acting out of instinct. Her surge of emotions–anger, frustration, pain–converged into one unified conglomerate, and the result was what the young woman sitting below at the park bench was witnessing.

The mother robin torpedoed into the body of the hawk, only to meet with the nonchalance of his stoic frame.

He didn't care. It was of no use.

Repeatedly she struck him, and repeatedly, he unflinchingly looked back at her, barely acknowledging her existence. That was all. There was no dent in his being. No damage to his core. There was no effect. Her actions were futile.

The mother robin finally let go. She gave up her course of action, and drifted slowly below the hawk, behind the tree, and disappeared into the far distance.

She was gone. And that was it.

The young woman sitting at the park bench below witnessed this entire drama unfold. Then, almost as if nature itself was trying to offer her a revelation, she realized something.

She realized how futile it is to be engaged with matters over which she has no control. All the anger, the disappointment, the fashioning and fathoming, will do nothing to change the past. But rather, it will do everything to change her present and her future. She would become a vengeful person, her heart would harden, incapable of letting love in once again. She would become someone she no longer recognized. A stranger would be staring back at her in the mirror.

This version of the future, she did not want. She realized at that moment, that she too, like the mother robin, must forgive and let go. Not for the sake of anyone else that had wronged her, and not even because they deserved it, but because she did. She deserved peace. She must let go for herself.

She knew that if she wanted to grow into the woman that destiny had called upon her to be, she would need to let go:

of everything she didn't want to be and the person she had been as of late. She had to let go of the pain, of the frustration. She had to let go of the anger and disappointment. She had to let go of the "could have been's" and the "should have been's." She had to let go of trying to understand things that she simply could not, and likely would never be able to. She had to let go of her past, in order to reclaim her present, and ultimately her future.

Like the mother robin, she had to understand that to hold onto pain and anger, is like holding onto a slowly-growing cancer that will only poison herself, and no one else. Not those who have wronged her, not those who have abandoned her, and not those who had failed to see the true value within her.

The past cannot be changed; it never can. The actions of others remain as real in her mind as the oak trees before her. She felt so close to them, but knew she would not and could not stay much longer. She had people to meet, goals to accomplish. Life was waiting for her; it had been waiting all along. And yet she hadn't realized it until now.

The past no longer had the same effect upon her, because she finally realized that others do not deserve that place in her life any longer. That influence over mind and emotion is a pure, beautiful, vulnerable thing. And she refused to allow anyone else to have that kind of power over these vulnerabilities. They did not deserve it. She understood what she could, acknowledged what she couldn't. And ultimately she let it all go, into the universe, into the cosmos. Into the horizon.

With the mother robin.

everything we fear

Maybe everything we fear the most,
just needs our patient
and nonjudgmental curiosity.

Maybe every once in a while,
we need to show ourselves
the same kind of loving kindness
we wish others show us.

The same love
we so long for
from another,
we must show
to ourselves,
first.

subject to interpretation

Far too often, we may think
others cause us to feel a certain way,
but it is really our interpretation
that does so.

Only you can give someone power
to make you feel something, anything.
And only you can take that power away
and give it back to its rightful owner: yourself.

Any response we have to a given event,
is based upon how we identify with
and orient ourselves towards that particular
event. To the parts of that event
that echo and reverberate within our soul.
The event does not shape us;
our worldview does.
Our soul does.

We define our own perspective;
the choice is ours.
Inner peace is everything.
So choose peace.

better place

The world is a better place now,
because you have made it so.

Even if no one knows, I do.
And so does the world.

today is a celebration

Today is a celebration of everything you've ever been through to get to this point in your life: all the steps you've taken, the challenges you have overcome, and the challenges that have overcome you.

You've been through it all, haven't you?

And yet here you are; not in spite of it all, *but because of it all*, because of everything you have been through. You needed to go through those experiences to be who you are today.

Today is a celebration of all the things you had to endure when you didn't think you had it in you: the good and the bad, the wins and the losses, the triumphs and defeats. They are all part of your story. And you know full-well that you are grateful for all of it, because you cannot pick and choose what you are grateful for. You cannot take the good without the bad (nor should you), just as you cannot take the bad without the good.

All of it is part of your story. It was always meant to be that way.

your shooting star

Sometimes you need to remember
that the shooting stars you see
in the middle of the night,
are there for you and only you.

They are wishing upon you too,
just as you wish upon them.

be patient

Be patient with yourself,
with everything
you are trying so hard to become.

Allow life to happen to you
and let it mold you
into the person
you are destined to be.

All things that are worth it, take time.
Even angels need time to grow their wings.

All things that are beautiful take time to reach
their full potential; not all things are meant to
happen quickly, but require patience and trust.

Patience to wait, and trust to know that whatever
the outcome, life is always in the right.

hold steadfast to the light

Connect and hold steadfast
to the light found within you.

And know that this light
will never lead you astray,
because it is of the world,
and belongs to all of existence:
everything that has come before you
and that which will come after you.
This light is found in all of it.

It will never lead you astray.

the comeback is always bigger

The comeback
is always bigger
than the setback.

...

The comeback is always stronger than the
setback, but only if you allow it to be. Setbacks
are opportunities for growth, for they carry
within them, lessons. In this way, they are
opportunities for you to redefine and reinvent
who you are–to change your blueprint, so to
speak.

And that's the thing about growth: you're never
quite the same person you once were.

the stars call for you

There are stars
out there
calling for you,
you have yet to discover.

And they know you by name.

greater things

There are far, far greater things ahead,
waiting for us,
than any and all of the things
that we have left behind.

Sometimes, we forget this to be true.

the unfolding

Allow life to unfold,
as it does,
as it will,
as it should.

And surrender
to the mystery
unfolding before you.

***

Sometimes, we get so caught up in taking
control, that we lose sight of the bigger picture.
We forget that there is only so much planning
we can do, before life takes over.

Half of the battle is already won when we realize
two fundamental truths: life will always unfold
as it should, and life is in the right, always.

So wherever we find ourselves, may we
remember to let go, and allow life simply to
transpire in all its beauty.

currency of grace

May we learn to recognize,
just as we do
the number of friends someone has
on *facebook*
or the number of likes a post receives
on *instagram*,
the inherent currency of grace
found within each one of us.

heart warrior

She was a heart warrior
in the truest sense of the word–
one of the last living semblances of her kind,
of what it means
to give your heart to another
and to watch it break,
repeatedly.
In a world full of paralytics
to quiet the thrashing,
she was not afraid to feel.
The scar tissue with its warped, iron-clad talons
only made her strong;
it only added to her resolve.
And all of the things most others feared,
feared to feel,
she became those very things.
There was no need to fear them any longer.
Fear lost its luster,
& metamorphosized into courage.
Because that's what courage is,
fear becoming conscious of itself.

the best teachers

The best teachers
ignite a flame within you,
a desire, a longing,
a purpose.

They breathe new life into you
so when you look upon the world,
you no longer see what you used to see,
or even what you want to see.

You see what you need to see.

over-complications

Sometimes, we tend to over-complicate
what is meant to be simple,
what is meant to be appreciated
and accepted without judgment.
We add layers to things
never meant to sustain
such a weight
or burden.

The simple cannot be,
nor should they be
adulterated.

It's sacrilege
on so many levels.

h^2

Heaven & hell
are not only the ends of a journey.
They exist in the present tense,
within the four corners of your mind.

With every thought, they find nourishment.
Like the origin of the cosmos,
energy and dust particles gather together
to create a nebulous, living, breathing being,
disguised as you,
within your thoughts.

You are your own heaven or hell.

the will of magic

You have to find a way
to let the magic inside of you, out.
Whatever the price.
However that may be.

As it is willed to be,
so shall it be.

the lucky ones

Here's the thing about luck that no one tells you:
those that are lucky, aren't really lucky.
Gamblers are lucky.

The lucky ones are blessed.
There's a big difference.

in the beginning // in the stillness

In the beginning,
long before the mind conceives it,
long before any words are uttered,
in the stillness of silence,
some gifts have already commenced
upon their journey to find you;
they are already on their way,
and have been for quite some time.

Some prayers are answered,
long before they are ever made.

And all that is ultimately meant for you,
will come into your life.
And that which isn't will leave.

The only lesson left to master
is to recognize when the time has come to let go,
and to receive.

wildest dreams

Because sometimes,
the beauty that life has to offer
is so beyond our wildest dreams,
that even the most artificial and complex
of intelligent designs,
meticulously churning through
every conceivable permutation of life's events,
can barely begin to fathom
the inherent beauty of such moments.

p.s.

P.S. Thank You,
from my new self
to my old self.
Because everything
I am today, I owe to
who I was back then.

Because my old self needed to happen,
for my current self to exist.

happenings (meant for us)

While it is true we tend to plan,
the greatest things in life,
beyond our most creative imaginings,
just sort of happen to us,

as if they were always meant for us...

And when asked about them,
we sit back, marvel, and say,
"I have no idea how any of this ever happened."

sacred space

There is a distance
between love and fear;
between who you are,
& who you wish to be.

And within this sacred space,
at the seat of your soul,
where love embraces fear
& hope greets anguish,
the mystery of who you are,
is where the truly eternal happens.

Where you can be present and feel
all of eternity in the bellows of
laughter and yearning just the same.

And it starts with your
freedom to choose.

god's creatures

Heaven holds a special place
for those who care for the most vulnerable
of God's creatures.

Adopt, don't shop.

biggest regrets

You will find,
your biggest regrets
will someday
be the reason for your greatest joys.

Only then will you rediscover
just how beautiful life can be.

everything, because

Everything...
  in its own time,
  in its own place,
  at its own pace,
  happens for a reason.

Because...
  you wouldn't know what to do with it
  had you found it any sooner.

Because...
  if you do get it,
  you would lose it.

Because...
  the things you've lost
  you were never truly meant to keep;
  and the things that stay,
  do so because they were made for you.
  They were meant for you.

the cradles of irony

And the greatest irony is this:
you cannot understand your past by reliving it.
It is only by living forward
that any sense can be made.
In this way, the knots of time
gently hold your entire lifeline in place.
And cradle you in your destiny.

the art of living

The art of living, because living is an art in itself, consists of a series of seemingly-arbitrary acts of holding on & letting go. Letting go of people, places, and ideas that no longer serve you, and holding steadfast to those that light the fire within you.

The stuff of love, compassion, healing, forgiveness, and joy.

And throughout the duration of these seemingly-coincidental occurrences of holding on & letting go, you find that they weren't really arbitrary after all.

There was a purpose, a reason to the ebb and flow. And just as the tide whisks away chunks and edges off a barrier reef, so too will you find in your distant future, that your greatest treasure lies in the parts within you that have stayed, forming a beautiful microcosm hidden beneath the ocean current that was always meant to be.

gains & losses

One day,
everything
you've ever wished to gain,
will become everything
you wish you lost
& never had
in the first place.

the right answers

That the answers will come to you
in the right time,
at the right place,
in the right moment,
when you're ready.
And only when you're ready.

Because if they came any sooner,
you wouldn't know what to do with them,
let alone
know they were the answers
you've been seeking
all along.

just static

The only person that matters is you.
The rest is just static.
White noise.
A futile attempt to fill the void with nothing,
until nothing is left.

aditi

The marvels of the beautiful henna design, the intricacies found within its convoluted pattern, is a kind of metaphor for life.

Just as the elaborately composed lines of the henna come together, intersect, come apart, and meet again, so too do the people, places, and phases of our lives.

People come into our lives and leave. And sometimes they stay. We go through phases that help transform who we are. We travel repeatedly within ourselves, shed away parts of who we are in the people and places we leave behind, and emerge as new beings, as new versions of ourselves. We may feel the same in the moment, but on some level we know we are forever changed.

The path may not always seem to make sense on its own, but taken as a whole, there is a rhyme and reason to the rise and fall of the lines. There is a purpose to the wholeness of life. And it's within these amazing complexities that our true humanity can be found.

i am

I am.
Because I'm here
and I matter.

11:11

The angels in your life
are here with you for a reason;
don't forget to thank them.
Their hearts beat in synchrony with yours.
Cry in unison with yours.
Love in unity with yours.
They are one with yours.

yesterday's sediments

I'm not who I was a year ago;
and nor do I wish to be.
Time has a way of settling the sediments,
until only the essential is left,
until only the truth is left behind,
until the truth is all that remains.

living and dying

On some level,
our lives are but a series of successive
deaths and rebirths.
We each die dozens of times
throughout our lives.
But it's those that truly learn from their
suffering, those that grow into it,
that grow through it,
that are reborn
into their authentic selves.
The rest just simply die
over and over again,
until nothing is left.

stuff of destiny

If time allows it to happen,
if the stars watching over you see it fit,
and the moon grins at the possibilities,
it's meant for you and only you;
it's the only way it could have ever been.
That's the stuff destiny is made of.

the comfort of the unknown

In confronting the unknown,
take comfort in knowing:
it really doesn't matter which path you choose.
There are no wrong twists & turns,
no flaws in the journey.

Because of the many roads you embark upon,
any and all of them will ultimately lead you
to the path you were meant to travel.

They always have,
and always will.

invest in tenderness

Mama said,
"just as man is capable
of death and destruction,
he is also capable of love and tenderness."

"Look there," she said. "Invest yourself there.
All of life can be explained in that."

the slow relearn

I'm slowly relearning
all of the things
I was forced to forget,
when trying
to be faithful to life,
or at least the way
I pictured it to be.

blm

Every once in a while, a pivotal moment arises when life grants us the opportunity to be good and to do right. These sorts of crossroads are few and far in between, but they occur nonetheless. And it is up to us not only to be aware of when these moments arise, but also why they occur, and to have enough moral courage to do what is right. To act in such a way so as to become who we want to become.

My prayer is that we are able to rise to this occasion, to rise above these ashes and be better versions of ourselves–for our sake and for our children's sake, so that we can leave this world better than we found it.

We cannot change who we were. We cannot change the past no matter how much we wish we could, but we can change who we will become. The future is yet unwritten. I pray that we choose love, each and every time. This is my short prayer.

destinations

The destination that you seek is here.
You've arrived.
You just didn't know it.
And all the times you felt
you were getting lost,
you were really being found.

the simplicity of belonging

It was simple,
really.
It never belonged to me
in the first place.
Nothing ever really belongs to you
in all honesty.
The tide comes and goes,
and brings
or takes away with it
what it may,
what it does,
what it should.

It never belonged to me;
it belonged to the ocean.

As do I.

lessons x lessons

There is not much I know about life for certain. In fact, there is very little I do know. I've tried to live each moment to the fullest. I've travelled to the lands of love and happiness, wishing to never leave. And I've frequented the deep, dark depths of despair and agony more than a few times, wishing only to leave those places but feeling at times unable to.

Here is all that I've learned:

I've learned that people will say they love you, but their actions may not align with their words. True love expresses true love. One begets the other. Anything less is not real love, but a quasi-selfish form-of-loving. Love is essentially selfless. It is devoid of pain. It is not meant to hurt. You are not meant to feel worthless. And if it does hurt–the pain is a sort of growth that you know is real growth, where the two of you are growing together into a stronger union. There is beauty in growth. It can be painful, but you feel the beauty, and recognize it as real growth.

I've learned that if you look closely enough, you can see someone's true colors. But you must watch, not necessarily listen. You do not need to listen. Just watch their actions. Watch what they do, and how they act towards you.

I've learned that when someone shows you who they are, believe them. And believe them the first time. You do not need to wait until they show you for the second, third, fourth, or fifth time. These are elements of their personality and they rarely change. So do yourself a favor and believe what they are trying to show you, for they are revealing who they truly are for your sake.

I've learned that if you are not kind to yourself, if you do not respect yourself and declare your boundaries–some will take advantage of you. Not all, but some. And they will do so because you allow them to; they do not know any better. So if others are treating you poorly and disrespecting you, it is because you are allowing them to. That is the message you are sending them.

So do yourself a favor and take care of you. Love yourself. Love who you are. Know that you are the most precious being you know. And realize that you deserve to be treated with love and respect. And when another shows you ugliness and pain, do not allow their pain and anguish to seep into your essence. Put a stop to it.

I've learned that some people are weak and insecure, and how they treat others is a reflection of how they treat themselves. The views they have of others are the same ones they share for themselves. The voice they use to address others, is the same they use to talk to themselves. So if anything, feel sorry for them, pray for them, for that is their world. Not yours. It is them; not you. They are the ones that are suffering, and their suffering is spilling over into you. Don't allow that to happen.

I've learned that life is always in the right. That there is a powerful being out there who is at work–molding you into the person that destiny has called upon you to be. So trust in that power, and know that whatever you are going through is meant for you, and is made for you; it is a step towards growth, and into becoming the person you are meant to become.

I've learned that this powerful being never gives you more that you can handle. You are going through it because this being has faith that you can overcome this challenge. You have what it takes within you to do so. So have faith in yourself and who you are. Live in the present moment. Just keep going. And trust in this powerful, all-knowing creator. Trust in life, for life is always happening for you, and not to you.

It is celebrating your existence, every time you die and are reborn. Because it knows that with each death and rebirth, you are becoming all that you were meant to be: a truer, more authentic, more vulnerable and more beautiful version of yourself.

gratitude for growth

I am grateful for the lessons I've learned, and the unconscious growth that has taken place within me. I am grateful that I found the strength to let go, so that I may flourish.

I am grateful that I was taught all the ways not to be loved, not to be appreciated, not to be admired–for in effect, I was taught what true love, admiration, and appreciation really are.

I am grateful for all that I've lost, for what never was, could never be.

And most of all, I am grateful for the caring and compassionate human I have become, and will always be–a person who refuses to allow the actions of those that are immature and insecure, to jeopardize, even for a moment, my recognition of the value that the good lord has blessed me with.

the prize & the process

The act is the prize.
No amount of fortune and fame
can take the place of the process.
It is essential,
irreplaceable.
The process is all there ever really is;
the journey upon which
all subsequent other journeys
are founded.

in search of meaning

We are at our best when we find time to introspect and create meaning from our lives; it is a natural inclination ingrained in our psyche. Just as we expect that the sun will rise in the morning, so too do we hope that we will discover meaning in the most obscure of experiences.

With that said, is it true that we only realize the value of something once it is gone? Is it possible to comprehend the significance of an experience while in the midst of that experience? To discover the full-breadth of feeling, emotion, insight, and fulfillment an event may incur upon our personhood during its transpiration? Or does it have to end for us to understand its importance in our lives? And the meaning created within our lives?

***

We are capable of creating meaning for ourselves during an event: of what that occurrence represents in our lives and worldviews, how it may change our perspective about ourselves, the world, and our place in it.

However, the meaning we may garner during or even right after an experience may not be of the same nature or quality as that which we may stumble upon during our subsequent years; it simply cannot be. That is, we may feel we have understood all there is to understand from a life occurrence–all the different ways in which the event may have molded us into the people we are today, all of the insights we've woven into the tapestries of love, and living purposefully– but we are likely only entertaining the superficial.

Much like a glacier floating at peace upon the crispness of the ocean, it takes those years, and that time after an experience to discover ultimately the significance of an event in our lives. Perhaps further knots must be tied in the strings of time to understand how the association of our experiences lends itself to a unified whole–a theme, if you will, that may be explored and understood. The existence and meaning of those knots is comprehensible in retrospect, but little do they accomplish with regards to reason during an experience.

And the most interesting of all, the meaning that is garnered as we live our lives is malleable. It is dynamic. As such, not only may we discover that we have uncovered greater depths to an experience's significance. We may also come to realize that the meaning we once held about an experience no longer applies, or has even changed.

Somewhere during the course of time, the tides have uncovered novelties that have influenced the quality of meaning to such a degree, and to such an extent, that it ceases to be what it once was. An even newer insight is garnered, and caught in the web of understanding. And this insight is what is often termed as a "revelation."

What once looked so stable and real, no longer is true, and makes way for a transformation so great that our will is tested, our understanding is intertwined with our destiny, and we feel an aura about ourselves so great we swear the angels in heaven can feel its incandescent glow upon their soft, gentle dispositions.

We suddenly have a greater comprehension; our souls are refreshed and reinvigorated. We feel the swelling of a spring in our center. Our inner self is at peace with our existence. We know why we are here, why we were placed on this earth.

As we may imagine, this process of "meaning-forging" is not an overnight occurrence. It may take years, perhaps even a lifetime, to transpire fully. As such, it is imperative that in addition to the practices of self reflection and "soul-searching," we be patient and open to all that is churning within our soul.

For the soul is hard at work, infinitely creating and destroying, forever living and dying, to create out of a series of seemingly incomprehensible experiences–a synergistic whole greater than the sum of its parts, a meaning of the stuff that can only be likened to divine intervention, a miracle, a revelation. And perhaps the most beautiful of all is still humanity's natural desire to search for and create meaning in life.

ABOUT THE AUTHOR

Sarkis Kavaris has been writing ever since he could remember; what once was a pastime hobby evolved into a true passion when he attended Georgetown University. It was there that he found his calling to be a writer; he frequently wrote and performed songs on his acoustic guitar at local coffee shops around the D.C. area. Writing became a way of life for him, an outlet to express the commonalities we all share as human beings, and the responsibility we each have in spreading goodness wherever life finds us. Writing has been his way of doing just that; it's been his answer to life's difficult questions. When he's not writing, he enjoys watching baseball, practicing Muy Thai, and meditating.

He currently resides in Los Angeles with his pet parrot *Dante*.

Made in the USA
Monee, IL
14 March 2021